A Young Citizen's Guide To:

The Criminal Justice System

Sean Sheehan

W

HODDER
Wayland

An imprint of Hodder Children's Books

A Young Citizen's Guide series

Parliament
Local Government
The Electoral System
Central Government
The Criminal Justice System
Voluntary Groups
The Media in Politics
The European Union
Political Parties
Money

© Copyright 2002 Hodder Wayland

Published in Great Britain in 2002 by Hodder Wayland, an imprint of Hodder Children's Books

Editor: Patience Coster
Series editor: Alex Woolf
Series design: Simon Borrough
Picture research: Glass Onion Pictures
Consultant: Dr Stephen Coleman
Artwork: Stefan Chabluk

British Library Cataloguing in Publication Data
   Sheehan, Sean, 1951-
   A young citizen's guide to the criminal justice system
   1. Criminal justice, Administration of - Great Britain -
   Juvenile literature
   I. Title II. The criminal justice system
   364'.0941

ISBN 0 7502 3778 3

Printed and bound in Hong Kong by C&C

Hodder Children's Books,
a division of Hodder Headline
Limited, 338 Euston Road,
London NW1 3BH

Picture acknowledgements:
the publisher would like to thank the following for permission to reproduce their pictures: Aerial Portraits/Impact 18 (top); Eye Ubiquitous 4 (G Daniels), 11 (G Daniels), 19 (Chris Fairclough), 26 (J Burke); Impact 21 and *title page* (Peter Arkell), 22 (Colin Jones), 24 (Lionel Derimais); Popperfoto 10 (Mike Fisher), 28; Popperfoto/Reuter 6 (Kieran Doherty); Press Association/Topham 12 (Stefan Rousseau), 13 (Brian Little), 14 (Tony Harris); Topham Picturepoint 8, 9 (bottom), 16, 20 (M Cleaver/STF), 25; Topham/Press Association 5 (Ian Nicholson), 7 (Matthew Fearn), 15 (Rebecca Naden), 18 (bottom) and *contents page* (Fiona Hanson), 27 (David Jones); Wayland Picture Library 9 (top).

Cover: policewoman (Camera Press/L Smillie); Judge's Breakfast at the Bar (Impact); the Scales of Justice at the Old Bailey (Impact); detention centre (Impact).

Contents

What is the Criminal Justice System?

In the UK, the criminal justice system (CJS) is the part of government responsible for investigating crimes, finding the people who have committed them and bringing them to justice. The CJS also works to rehabilitate criminals after they have been punished, and helps the victims of crime. It is made up of a large number of organizations, namely:

- the police – who investigate crimes, arrest suspects and collect evidence;
- the Crown Prosecution Service (CPS) – which studies the details of criminal cases investigated by the police and decides whether to prosecute someone or not;
- the judiciary – a system of courts in which criminal cases are heard;
- the probation service – which helps ex-offenders return to normal society and tries to make sure they do not commit any further crimes;
- the Serious Fraud Office – which investigates fraud;
- the Criminal Defence Service – which provides legal assistance to all defendants;
- the Criminal Injuries Compensation Authority – which awards compensation (often a sum of money) to people who have been injured or harmed as the result of a crime. This compensation is a way of making amends to the person who has suffered the crime.

The criminal justice system is responsible for finding and bringing to justice all kinds of criminals, from car thieves (below) to murderers.

The criminal justice system aims to reduce crime and to limit the fear of crime and the economic damage it causes. It seeks to protect the rights both of victims and of the people who commit crimes, and tries to see that justice is administered fairly. The CJS is a huge and vitally important part of society. If it fails, or if people begin to think it is corrupt or unfair, the basis of our peaceful lives may be seriously affected.

Who runs the criminal justice system?

Three different government departments are responsible for running the criminal justice system. These are the Home Office, the Attorney General's Office, and the Lord Chancellor's Department. The Home Office is responsible for the police, prisons and the probation service (see page 23). The Attorney General's Office is responsible for the CPS, which oversees nearly all the criminal cases investigated by the police. (The CPS is headed by the Director of Public Prosecutions.) The Lord Chancellor's Department deals with matters relating to the judiciary, in other words all the courts and judges in the UK. It runs the higher courts, which are where the more serious cases, such as murder, are heard. Local authorities run magistrates' courts, following guidelines set out by the Lord Chancellor's Department. The Lord Chancellor is head of the judiciary and responsible for the appointment of judges.

Lord Irvine of Lairg, the Lord Chancellor, is responsible for the organization and running of the UK's courts.

(see page 23)

'Fairness and justice are inseparable, and a major task for the criminal justice system is to ensure full equality of treatment for all.'
The Rt Hon Lord Justice Rose, Chairperson of the Criminal Justice Consultative Committee.

The criminal process

The laws of the United Kingdom are divided into criminal law and civil law. Criminal law concerns a crime against the state or individuals or property. Civil law deals with relations between individuals in, for example, contracts, or when someone damages another person's reputation. When someone breaks one of the criminal laws – whether it be going over the speed limit in a car, robbing a bank or carrying out a murder – a crime has been committed.

Once a crime has been committed, the police become involved. They investigate the crime and try to collect enough evidence to show that there is a case to answer. (The Crown Prosecution Service must prove in a courtroom that there are enough grounds to prosecute the person suspected of committing a crime. If they can do this, then there is 'a case to answer'.) After consulting the CPS, the police arrest the person suspected of committing the crime and may have the authority to hold him or her in prison until trial. At this stage, the CPS takes over and decides what crimes the suspect can be charged with. The suspect then has the charges (the list of suspected crimes) formally read to him or her. These charges are heard either in a magistrates' court, if the crime is a relatively minor one, or in the Crown Court, if the crime is more serious.

Policemen arrest a person suspected of a crime.

A magistrates' court. In 1999-2000, magistrates' courts in England and Wales heard 1.88 million cases.

The magistrates' court consists of two or three magistrates who decide whether the suspect (the defendant) is innocent or guilty. Magistrates are citizens who usually do not have a background in the legal profession. The Crown Court is made up of a judge and a jury of twelve members of the public. The jury hears the evidence and decides whether the defendant is innocent or guilty. When a decision has been reached, the judge decides on an appropriate punishment, called in the courts a 'sentence'.

There is a higher court, called the appeal court, where the convicted person's lawyers can appeal against the decision of the jury (known as the 'conviction'), or against the sentence. If the appeal fails, the lawyers can take the case to the House of Lords, which is the final court of appeal against a conviction in the UK. Beyond that, if the lawyers can prove that the defendant's human rights have not been respected, an appeal can be made to the European Court of Human Rights (ECHR).

Criminal justice in Scotland
The criminal justice system in Scotland is quite different from the system in England and Wales. Scottish law distinguishes between 'summary' and 'solemn' prosecutions. These are roughly equivalent to magistrates' and Crown Court cases. In Scotland, the lower courts (the sheriff courts) can hear either type of case, while the higher courts hear only solemn cases. Whether it is in the sheriff court or the high court, a jury of fifteen people always hears solemn cases. Unlike magistrates, sheriffs are professional judges. In Scotland, the jury has three choices of verdict – guilty, not guilty and not proven. The high court also acts as the court of appeal.

Once the courts have convicted a person, the prison or probation service becomes involved (see page 21).

The courts and the legal system often deal with civil law, where no crime has been committed but there is a dispute between citizens. Such matters include divorce cases, custody cases (between parents concerning who should look after the children after a divorce or separation), and libel cases (where someone claims that another person has damaged their reputation and demands compensation from them).

The Human Rights Act
In October 2000, the Human Rights Act became law in the UK. Since the 1950s, many people have challenged UK law in the European Court on the grounds that it conflicts with their human rights. Since 2000, all British laws must be looked at closely in case they go against the Human Rights Act, which guarantees rights of freedom. These rights include free assembly (the right to meet together in public), free speech (the right to express your opinions publicly), a fair trial, the right to privacy, education, and birth control, freedom from torture, slavery and racial discrimination. The new Human Rights Act should mean that UK citizens no longer have to undergo the expense and difficulty of an appeal to the European Court of Human Rights.

Circuit court judges. The Crown Court consists of six court 'circuits'. Each circuit is made up of different areas of England and Wales and has a major city as its administrative centre. The circuit courts try cases in the area in which the defendant was first formally charged by a magistrate.

The Police and the Crown Prosecution Service

As long ago as the twelfth century, towns and villages made their own arrangements for keeping the peace. Watchmen were employed by the local authorities to patrol the streets at night. Their duty was to keep order and they

had wide-ranging powers to lock up unruly citizens. In 1828 the Home Secretary, Sir Robert Peel, set up Britain's first organized police force in London. Other towns and cities followed suit, and it was only in the 1960s that the hundred or more local police forces were merged into just over forty.

By the middle of the twentieth century, the role of the police had expanded enormously to include many of its modern functions, for example, crime investigation and prevention, traffic control, specialist firearms units, dog handling and more. This growth in responsibilities brought with it an enormous increase in the power of the police and a corresponding need for stricter government control over how they operated.

Above: a watchman's job was to mark the hours with his bell, report on fires, guard the city gates, light the lamps and report any disorder. Watchmen patrolled the streets of England's towns and cities until 1829.

Right: in days gone by, the typical British 'bobby' could be seen helping children to cross the street safely.

Gathering evidence

By the 1980s there were serious concerns about policing in the UK, especially about the way in which prosecutions were brought to court. Then the police had responsibility both for gathering evidence and for deciding to prosecute a suspect. This practice was believed by some to be open to abuse. They argued that the police were in a position in which they could tamper with evidence to bring about a successful conviction. In 1985 the Crown Prosecution Service was set up to separate the gathering of evidence from the decision to prosecute someone. As an independent body, it looks at the evidence impartially before a decision to prosecute is made. This change has caused concern among some police officers. They feel that they can no longer see their work through to the end and are only connected to the outcome of an arrest if they are called to give evidence at a trial.

In 1975, four Irish people were convicted of planting a bomb in a pub in Guildford. In 1989, the Guildford Four's conviction was overturned because of doubtful evidence produced at the trial and they were released from prison (above).

A changing police service

Today, only one in four reported crimes is solved, and there is continued concern about the way in which policing is carried out in the UK. There is currently much discussion in the police service itself about its role and function. Because of the huge demands that modern society makes on police time and resources, many police forces feel under pressure to reject the traditional foot patrols in favour of rapid response units – police in cars who can respond quickly to incidents. In the past, members of the local police force were readily recognizable within their neighbourhoods, but now many communities see the police as remote

'[The CPS are] not an efficient service because they're not policemen. People say we should be detached, but when you've arrested somebody right at the scene of the crime and you've seen the results of their behaviour, you cannot be otherwise than personally involved and think, "They should be put away". Someone who comes in at nine in the morning, into an office, has got nothing at all to do with the police force and meeting the people who are hit by the crime.'

A policeman's view of the Crown Prosecution Service, quoted in *Talking Blues: The Police in Their Own Words* by Roger Graef.

and anonymous individuals. This means that the police service, which once relied on local information given to the local constable, now depends heavily on modern technology, like closed circuit television (CCTV) cameras.

The work of the police

A 1993 report stated that over 60 per cent of all calls to the police are not connected with any crime, but are about things like noisy neighbours, lost property and missing persons. The police deal with motoring offences, the monitoring of events like football matches and demonstrations, and the investigation of crimes. There is a two-tier system of policing in Britain: local police stations deal with locally reported crimes, while major crime investigations such as those into organized crime and large-scale drug dealing are carried out by the National Criminal Intelligence Service, an organization that is independent of the local police.

Police today use rapid response units – fast-moving cars that enable them to arrive at the scene of a crime quickly. These policemen are carrying guns and wearing body armour to deal with a dangerous situation.

Sexism and racism The police service also suffers from a lack of new recruits among women and ethnic minorities. A traditional male culture within the force, and the charge that people from ethnic minorities are not treated fairly by the police mean it is difficult to create a police force that reflects contemporary society. In the 1990s, the failure of the police to prosecute anyone in the case of the racist murder of black teenager Stephen Lawrence led to the Macpherson Report into the London police. The report concluded that the force suffered from institutional racism. This meant that racist attitudes were deeply rooted in the culture of the police service and were not simply the result of individuals who happen to be racist.

In Northern Ireland the police service has experienced special problems arising from the need to police a community divided between Catholics and Protestants. Most members of the existing police force come from the Protestant community. A recent inquiry urged the creation of a more balanced police force.

On a more positive note, the police service is well aware of its problems, many of which have been caused by the massive increase in its responsibilities over the years. It is quick to respond in a positive way to criticism and reforms are under way in the Metropolitan police and in the police service in Northern Ireland.

Women police officers make up just 16 per cent of the police force of England and Wales. There are slightly fewer women police officers in Scotland and Northern Ireland.

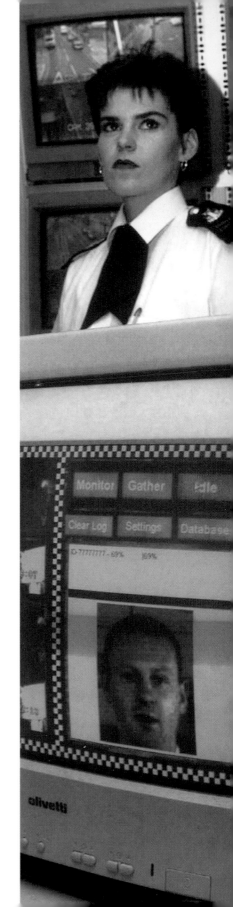

The Stephen Lawrence case
In April 1993, a young sixth-form student, Stephen Lawrence, was murdered in a racist attack in south London. The police handling of the case – which included their failure to make early arrests and their treatment of the bereaved family – was criticized in the 1999 Macpherson Report. The report concluded that: 'Unwitting racism can arise because of lack of understanding, ignorance or mistaken beliefs.... It can arise from unfamiliarity with the behaviour or cultural traditions of people or families from minority ethnic communities. It can arise from racist stereotyping of black people as potential criminals or troublemakers... such attitudes can thrive in a tightly knit community, so that there can be a collective failure to detect and to outlaw this breed of racism. The police canteen can too easily be its breeding ground.'

The Royal Ulster Constabulary presents many problems to the peace process in Northern Ireland. The recommendations for its reform have pleased neither the Catholic nor the Protestant communities.

The Crown Prosecution Service

There are forty-two divisions of the CPS across the UK. Each one has its own chief prosecutor and a team of lawyers and clerical staff. They examine the evidence collected by the police and decide whether or not a prosecution should be made. If the evidence seems too flimsy, or if there is thought to be less than a 50 per cent chance of a successful prosecution, the CPS will not go ahead. A case may also be abandoned if the accused is too old or ill to stand trial. Certain types of cases may be considered too numerous or too insignificant to bother with. If, for example, the CPS pursued every minor drug charge, the courts would have to spend a lot of valuable time dealing with these.

The parents of Stephen Lawrence (far left of picture) brought a private prosecution for murder against three men after the CPS, on the grounds of insufficient evidence, had chosen not to prosecute. The Lawrence's case failed.

If the CPS wants to bring charges of terrorism or offences against the Official Secrets Act, it must get the permission of the Attorney General. The Attorney General is the UK's most senior legal officer and the person appointed to act as legal representative of the state. In special circumstances, the Attorney General may stop trials that the CPS is prosecuting if, for example, they are seen to have become too sensitive or notorious. In 1998, the Attorney General stopped the trial of author Tony Geraghty which had become controversial because there wasn't a case to answer (see opposite). Other bodies can also bring prosecutions: they include the Inland Revenue, the Serious Fraud Office and the Department of Social Security. Private citizens can also bring their own prosecutions.

The CPS has independent monitoring inspectors who check for good practice within the criminal justice system. This includes monitoring the way in which ethnic minorities are treated by a court system that in 1996 only drew 1.6 per cent of its more senior legal staff from Britain's ethnic minorities.

'It has not been easy, especially since we started with only twelve modern computers/PCs between 150-plus staff; part of my job has been to modernize the service. We're also trying to improve the CPS's approach to equality and diversity, not just in terms of recruitment, but also in disseminating information and being more open and accessible....
Though I don't know for sure, I think I'd probably earn a fair bit more doing a similar job in the private sector, or even the police or probation service. When I joined the service fifteen years ago, it was just a job to me, but after all this time I now have a real personal investment in the work, so it has turned into something I'm very committed to getting right.'
A worker in the CPS describes his job.

Examining the Evidence: the Courts

Magistrates' courts have existed for more than 600 years. Some 95 per cent of criminal cases are heard in these courts. Three magistrates head each court. There are about 30,000 non-professional magistrates in England and Wales and a further one hundred legally-trained, professional magistrates who hear more complex trials. The less serious crimes, such as petty theft, minor motoring offences and vandalism, are heard by magistrates. In most cases, the defendant pleads guilty and the magistrates' main job is to pass sentence, which may be up to a maximum of six months in prison.

Trial by jury In some cases, such as assault, burglary, theft and dangerous driving, the defendant who chooses to plead not guilty can opt for a jury trial. In 2000, the Labour government introduced a bill in Parliament to drop this option, leaving the magistrates to decide whether the accused has the right to a trial by jury. Many people involved in the legal profession see this as an erosion of people's rights. In Scotland, the police decide which type of court a defendant should be prosecuted in.

Tony Geraghty, author of the book *The Irish War*, was put on trial in 1998 for revealing information about computer software used by British military intelligence in Northern Ireland. The Attorney General first approved the case, then dismissed it on the grounds that there wasn't a case to answer.

For and against the right to choose a trial by jury

Against
- most people who opt for a jury trial change their minds later and plead guilty, wasting time and money
- Crown Court judges pass heavier prison sentences than magistrates
- some £40 million per year would be saved by removing the option to choose
- the option allows criminals to play the system – they may choose a jury trial in the hope that, because of the length of time that passes before it can take place, witnesses might have died or gone abroad, or for some other reason may not be available once the trial gets under way.

For
- because most magistrates are white, defendants from ethnic minorities may feel they are at a disadvantage. In a jury trial it is likely that they will be judged by a more representative section of multicultural Britain
- 65 per cent of jury trials end in a not guilty verdict. The defence lawyers will advise their client that he or she has a better chance of being acquitted in the Crown Court
- a jury trial benefits the defendant because the defence lawyer's fee is paid by the state in the Crown Court, but is rarely paid by the state in a magistrate's court
- magistrates take a person's character into account, juries don't. People with a difficult past may have that held against them in a magistrates' court. In a Crown Court the jury will not hear about it.

An artist's impression of a trial in a Crown Court. In the foreground sits the defendant, guarded by police. The judge sits above the main body of the room (in the background of this picture). In front of the judge is the court recorder. The prosecution and defence counsels are positioned between the recorder and the defendant.

Bail Magistrates decide if defendants should be released on bail while awaiting trial. Bail is a legal term which means that the defendant promises to return for his or her trial at a later date. The defendant usually has to find a large sum of money, which the court can take if he or she fails to turn up when told to do so.

Magistrates also head youth courts for defendants under the age of eighteen. The purpose of these courts is to ensure that young offenders receive sentencing as soon as possible after their crime. Experts believe that young criminals should be tried quickly so that they understand the link between their crime and the punishment they receive, and that they should be spared the long wait to find out what will happen to them. Unlike local magistrates' courts, youth courts are not open to the public.

The Crown Court Criminal cases that are considered too serious to be heard in a magistrates' court go to the Crown Court. These courts have existed since 1972. Crimes such as murder, rape, arson, armed robbery and fraud are heard in the Crown Courts. A single, professional judge holds the court. His or her role is to oversee matters of law and to pass sentence if necessary. The case is presented to the jury, members of the public who have been summoned to hear the case and decide whether the defendant is guilty or not guilty.

In 2001, the teenagers suspected of murdering a primary school boy, Damilola Taylor, arrive at West London youth court to hear the charges brought against them.

Only about a third of cases brought before Crown Courts are heard by juries. Roughly two-thirds of all cases appear only for sentencing, because the defendant enters a guilty plea. Of those that are tried by jury, more than half are found not guilty. There are ninety Crown Courts in England and Wales and each has several courtrooms. The most famous of them all is the Central Criminal Court, built on the site of Newgate prison, and also known as the Old Bailey.

Apart from the judge and the jury, there are many more people involved in Crown Court cases. A court recorder sits in front of the judge's seat and records what is said. Ushers and a clerk of the court call witnesses, look after the jury, and handle the evidence. Barristers, people qualified in law, who have been called to the bar (that is, given permission to practise law in the Crown Court), represent the prosecution and the defendant. Like the judge, they wear wigs and gowns and conduct their business in very polite language, calling one another 'my learned friend' and the judge 'm'lud' or 'm'lady'. In English courts, barristers are pitted against

The figure of justice stands on top of the Old Bailey, a famous Crown Court building in London.

Patricia Scotland, Britain's first black woman barrister. Today 46 per cent of barristers are women, compared with only 8 per cent in 1972.

one another. The two barristers sit at separate tables, and the defendant's solicitor and the solicitor of the CPS sit behind them.

The appeal process
After a judgement has been made, the defendant can appeal against it. Appeals against verdicts or sentences made in magistrates' courts go to the Crown Court. Here a judge, often sitting with two magistrates, reviews all the evidence in the case. Crown Court convictions go to the appeal court, where two or three judges review the trial. The judges may order a retrial, alter the sentence or have the accused released from prison. Judgement is by majority decision, which means that only two of the three judges have to agree on it. There are thirty-five appeal court judges, headed by the Lord Chief Justice.

Sometimes a case goes beyond the appeal court to the Law Lords in the House of Lords. These are twelve judges who are called on to make decisions regarding very complex criminal cases. Their decision often alters the way in which laws are interpreted. When a case is taken to the Law Lords, five of them review it and judgement is by majority decision. Many people believe that this second court of appeal is unnecessary and expensive and sometimes results in dubious decisions. For example, in 1998 the Law Lords' decided that the ex-dictator of Chile, General Pinochet, should be sent to Spain to answer charges of crimes against humanity. Their decision was queried when one of the Law Lords was found to have a connection with the prosecutors of the case.

'Once the trial is over it's dissolved, and there is no person responsible to anybody or answerable for the decision. It can therefore be much more independent. It hasn't got to consider what people might think of it as an individual.'
A Crown Court judge on the advantages of the jury system, quoted in *The Law Machine* by Marcel Berlins and Clare Dyer.

The Royal Courts of Justice in Westminster, London. Its business is mainly with civil cases, but it occasionally deals with criminal trials.

There is no appeal process for not guilty verdicts. A defendant who has been found not guilty cannot be retried for the same crime. This is known as the rule of 'double jeopardy'. Since the collapse of the trial against the men accused of killing Stephen Lawrence, moves are taking place to change this law where, say, DNA evidence later proves that the defendant is definitely guilty.

The trial of the children who murdered James Bulger aroused public anger. Here police restrain members of a crowd watching the accused arrive at court.

The James Bulger murder trial

British law allows children as young as ten years old to be tried as adults if the offence is serious enough. When the toddler James Bulger was murdered by two ten-year-olds, they were tried in an adult court. They were sentenced to an indefinite stay in prison. This meant they would remain in prison until the Home Secretary decided that their punishment was complete. In December 1999 the two boys' lawyers took their appeal to the European Court of Human Rights. The court found that the trial had been unfair because the boys were too young to understand the proceedings of the court. It ruled that a maximum sentence should be set. After the trial, one of the jurors said that the boys should have been found 'guilty as frightened and largely unaware children who made a terrible mistake and who are now in urgent need of psychiatric and social help'.

Punishment and Rehabilitation

Britain has used imprisonment as a method of punishment for about two hundred years. Before this, criminals were transported to one of the British colonies in Australia or America, or executed. By the late nineteenth century, Britain's prisons had been shifted from local authority to government control, and had become the most common means of punishment for convicted criminals.

In 1991 a law made it possible for prisons to be run independently of government. Now twelve of the 151 prisons in the UK are profit-making, privately-run institutions. In 2001, the number of people in prison in England and Wales totalled 65,460. These people are held in a range of high security and local prisons, remand centres and young offenders' institutions. Some recent reports on the state of UK prisons have criticized many of them for overcrowding, not dealing with bullying, and other failings.

Imprisonment is a well-established means of crime prevention. But many working in the CJS believe that prison helps offenders to develop their criminal skills.

Parole Unless they misbehave, most prisoners are given parole after serving two-thirds of their sentence. Most can apply for parole after a third of their sentence is completed. Parole means being released on licence, so that if prisoners re-offend they are brought back to prison. Those prisoners serving life sentences (usually twenty-five years) or indefinite sentences (where no time limit has been set on the length of time they must stay in prison) can only be released by permission of the Home Secretary. In the case of Myra Hindley, who was jailed in 1966 for the torture and murder of children, there is very little chance that she will ever be released, despite the fact that she has served more than twenty-five years of her life sentence.

In 1998 there were 65,300 people in prison in the UK, the highest number ever recorded.

Reform or punishment? Many

professionals working in the system believe that prison merely helps offenders to improve their criminal skills. This, and the fact that many prisoners feel that society has no use for them nor they for it, does not help to reduce crime rates. An interesting case in point is that of the two children convicted of murdering James Bulger. Aged ten at the time, the two boys were sent to a young offenders' institution. As they approached adulthood, the state had to make the choice either of sending them to an adult prison and into a criminal environment, or releasing them to see if they could lead normal lives. The decision was taken to release the boys under new identities in the hope that they will adjust to normal life.

Probation
An alternative punishment for convicted offenders is a period of probation. When sentenced to probation, an offender must not move away from home, and must report regularly to his or her probation officer and avoid any criminal associations. Probation usually involves attending a day centre where the offender learns skills such as anger management and discusses the damage that his or her crime has caused. If the offender breaks the rules that are set, he or she can be brought back to court and re-sentenced.

The probation service was started in the early twentieth century as a charity that helped released prisoners to become law-abiding citizens. Since then, its role has changed completely. The service now advises magistrates and judges on sentencing, oversees the offender's probation order and tries to reduce the rate of re-offending. Some probation officers work within the prison service, helping offenders who are about to be released, and assessing prisoners to see if they are suitable for early release or parole.

Young offenders' institutions
In 1997, after an investigation into the prison system, Sir David Ramsbotham, the Chief Inspector of Prisons, had the following to say about young offenders' institutions: 'Of all parts of the prison system, this is the one that needs the most attention. These are the young, impressionable people with their lives in front of them. Either we do nothing, in which case they'll continue to offend and be predators on society, or do something and hope that they mend their ways.' In a further investigation into Feltham Young Offenders' Institution in London in 1999 he described the prison as 'institutional deprivation' and 'rotten to the core'.

A changing role

Between 2000 and 2001, the probation service supervised an estimated 223,000 convicted people. Over the years, the age of those under the supervision of the probation service has risen, as has the number of people who have previously been in prison. Where once the probation service only looked after first-time young offenders, its job increasingly concerns the supervision of people convicted of fairly serious crimes such as robbery and burglary. Some 80 per cent of people on probation are unemployed, 50 per cent have drug-related problems and a small proportion have mental health problems. Despite this, over 80 per cent of probation orders are completed without the offender committing another crime. While it costs £34,000 to keep a person in prison for a year, a probation order costs £2,500. Some people see probation as a soft option, but statistics show that it is a far more effective way of preventing criminals from re-offending than a prison sentence.

Alternatives to prison

Prisons are expensive to run, overcrowded, and rarely have the resources to help prisoners deal with the kind of problems, such as drug addiction or unemployment, that often led them to commit crimes. Alternatives to prison relieve the pressure on the prisons and, in some cases, offer a more suitable method of punishment. They include:

- Community service orders – a court may sentence an offender to between 40 and 240 hours of community service. The offender undertakes unpaid tasks such as painting, renovating or environmental work. The offender loses leisure time and makes up for his or her crime. With community service, offenders face the challenge of working towards a goal and

This person who is out of prison on parole has agreed to wear an electronic tagging device so that his whereabouts are known at all times.

getting on with the other people in the project. Community service is often combined with a probation order, so that the offender also has the benefit of a probation officer to help him or her stay out of trouble.

- Curfew orders – the offender (often someone released early from prison) is required to wear an electronic tag. He or she has to spend certain hours at a given address. Any breaking of the curfew is picked up by electronic equipment.

Community service can provide an alternative to prison. In the USA, offenders shovel snow as part of an 'alternative incarceration program'.

Minorities in the criminal justice system

Ethnic minorities make up about 6 per cent of the population of the United Kingdom. A 1998 survey found that ethnic minorities made up the following percentages of the workforce in the criminal justice system:

- 5 per cent of solicitors
- 9 per cent of barristers
- 6.5 per cent of newly appointed magistrates
- 3 per cent of clerks of the court
- 8 per cent of probation officers
- 7 per cent of magistrates' court staff
- 2 per cent of police
- 2.73 per cent of prison officers
- 1.4 per cent of senior prison staff
- 4 per cent of Crown Court judges
- 0 per cent of the Law Lords

In a 1997 survey, 18 per cent of male prisoners and 25 per cent of female prisoners in England and Wales were from ethnic minorities.

- Drug treatment – if they agree to it, people convicted of drug offences may be sentenced to drug rehabilitation where they undergo a period of time in an addiction clinic. After their treatment, they can be tested for drugs for up to three years, and if traces of drugs are found they can be brought back to court for re-sentencing.

- Fines – courts can fine offenders for any crime, apart from murder and manslaughter. The courts have considerable powers to collect fines and people who do not pay are sent to prison. Courts usually take into account the ability of the offender to pay a fine before passing one as a sentence.

The Essex Motor Project
The typical Essex car criminal is male, teenage and began stealing cars at around the age of fourteen. By the time the criminal reaches the age of eighteen, he has already been in youth custody and is disqualified from driving. Because he can't drive legally or afford car insurance, he may steal cars in order to satisfy his addiction. In the Essex Motor Project, set up in 1993, teenagers that the probation service believes will respond to the treatment are sentenced to spend time at a local centre. Here they are counselled in victim awareness, decision-making and self-esteem and learn car mechanics and safe driving skills. The cars they work on are prepared for banger-racing and the best student of each session is allowed to drive in a banger race. Those who do not offend for six months after the probation order are offered third party insurance at normal rates. Since the project began, car crime in Essex has fallen below the national average.

This young man is taking part in a scheme similar to the Essex Motor Project. He learns to respect and handle cars, skills which will hopefully keep him from re-offending.

You and the Criminal Justice System

Most of us will come into contact with the criminal justice system at some time in our lives, either as victims, defendants, witnesses, jurors, or through our work. All UK citizens over the age of eighteen, apart from those with a criminal record or a history of mental illness, are eligible for jury service.

Victims of crime have the right to be treated with respect by the police and to be informed on the progress of their case. In court, they have the right to express how the crime has affected them. Particularly vulnerable victims do not have to face the accused in court. Suspects, defendants and offenders also have rights. The police cannot stop and search suspects without good grounds for suspicion. A suspect has a right to silence (although this can now be taken as a suggestion of guilt). Interviews with the police must be taped. The defendant has a right to see all the evidence collected by the police.

This woman has suffered a criminal attack and is recovering in hospital. But when her injuries have healed she will still carry the memory of what was done to her.

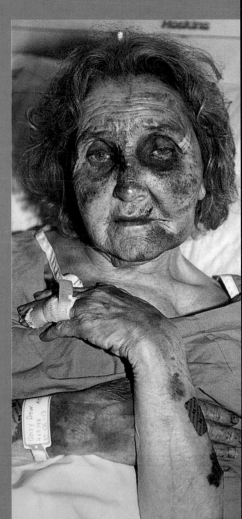

The cost of a trial by jury
Jury trials are expensive. The cost includes the salaries of those who work in the court, the expenses of the jury, the cost of expert witnesses, the cost of probation officers' and police work, and much more. The defendant also needs a defence team and perhaps expert witnesses or laboratory expenses. Most defendants could not possibly afford to pay for their own defence and in 95 per cent of jury trials the cost of the defence is found with legal aid, financed by the state.

Activity

One way of examining how it feels to be involved in the criminal justice system is to set up a Crown Court in your classroom. Follow the plan of the courtroom opposite to find out where judge, jury, defendant etc. sit. First of all, select twelve jury members and ask them to leave the room. Then follow the suggested scenario, below.

The crime

Six men armed with sawn-off shotguns enter a bank while a cash delivery is being made. They overpower the guards, injuring one of them seriously, and escape in a stolen car which is later found abandoned and burnt out. The men are recorded on CCTV but cannot be identified because they are wearing balaclavas and gloves. One of them speaks with a Scottish accent. They escape with £50,000 in new notes, which begin to appear in the cash registers of shops a few weeks later.

While reviewing an electrical superstore's CCTV, police officers spot the wife of a convicted bank robber, Gregory McTavish, passing one of the notes. They go to his house and arrest him. The search of his house unearths six balaclavas, six sets of gloves, a lot of new appliances, but no stolen money. Five of McTavish's friends say they were watching TV with him at the time of the robbery. None of the bank staff can identify McTavish, although he fits the height and build description of the man who spoke in a Scottish accent. McTavish is from Glasgow. In a later case, Mick Turner, a convicted gun dealer, tells the police that he sold six sawn-off shotguns to McTavish on the Sunday afternoon before the robbery occurred.

You will need the following characters:
- a defendant: Gregory McTavish
- a defence team
- a prosecuting team
- a judge
- a court recorder (to note down everything that is said in court so it can be read back later, if necessary)

- a court usher (to call the witnesses and look after the jury)
- bank staff and security men
- Mick Turner (currently in prison)
- arresting officers
- any defence witnesses

Remember the following
- you cannot use 'hearsay' evidence (in other words, you cannot repeat something you were told by someone else)
- the barristers cannot 'lead' the witness (for example, they must not say: 'Did you see Mr McTavish in the bank on the day of the robbery?' Rather they must say: 'What did you see on the day of the robbery?')
- the prosecution witnesses are examined first
- the defence witnesses are examined second
- the two sets of barristers sum up
- the jury members are not allowed to know about the defendant's past crimes
- the judge advises the jury
- the jury decides

McTavish and his defence team should refer to page 31 for further information.

You could make the Crown Court in your classroom look something like this.

Judge

Witness Box

Clerk of the Court and Usher

Recorder

Public Gallery

Defence

Prosecutor

Defence Solicitor

Prosecutor's Assistants

Jury

Accused

Glossary

acquitted found innocent by a jury

arson deliberately setting fire to a building

Attorney General the chief law officer of the state

barrister a lawyer who has been 'called to the bar'. Barristers are usually the only people who can prosecute or defend a case in the Crown Court

CCTV closed circuit television

constable a police officer below the rank of sergeant

curfew order a form of parole where the offender must be at home within certain hours

defendant the person in court accused of a crime

Department of Social Security the government department that handles assistance to people on low incomes

DNA evidence evidence provided by human cells left behind at a crime scene

double jeopardy the legal doctrine that no person can be tried twice for the same crime or for different crimes arising from the same set of facts

erosion wearing away

expert witness a qualified person, for example a doctor, who gives their opinion on a case heard in court

fraud cheating in order to make money

high security prison a prison where dangerous criminals are kept

Home Secretary the government minister in charge of police, prisons and probation service

impartiality not taking sides in a dispute

independent body an organization that is not financially or morally dependent on anyone else

Inland Revenue the government tax office

Law Lords twelve judges who sit in the House of Lords and can be called on to act as the final court of appeal in legal matters

legal aid legal help, usually the services of a solicitor, for someone charged with a crime

legislation a law

local authorities the government departments that oversee local areas

Lord Chief Justice the head of all the judges in the Crown and appeal courts

male culture a working environment dominated by men

metropolitan police the London police force

National Criminal Intelligence Service a service dedicated to fighting the most serious crimes

Official Secrets Act a law preventing people with information that might harm UK security from making it public

probation order an order by a judge for an offender to spend a period of time on probation

prosecute to bring criminal or civil charges against someone in a court of law

prosecutor the barrister who presents the case against a defendant in court

rehabilitate to help a person who has, for example, been injured or in prison settle back into normal life

remand centre a prison where charged suspects are kept until their trial or until they are allowed to leave on bail

re-offend to commit another crime

Serious Fraud Office a branch of the CJS which investigates cheating in business

solicitor a lawyer who works in an office and deals with most legal work outside of the Crown Court. They represent people in the magistrates' court. In 2000 the law was changed to allow some solicitors to work in the Crown Court.

suspect a person who the police think may have committed a crime

transported sent to one of the British colonies as a punishment

verdict the decision of the jury at the end of a trial

young offender institution a prison for people who are under the age of eighteen

Resources

Information books

Marcel Berlins and Clare Dyer, *The Law Machine*, Penguin, 2000

Brian Cathcart, *The Case of Stephen Lawrence*, Penguin, 2000

Roger Graef, *Talking Blues: The Police in Their Own Words*, Collins, 1989

Delores D Jones-Brown, *Race, Crime and Punishment*, Chelsea House Publications, 2000

David Wilson and John Ashton, *Crime and Punishment*, Blackstone Press, 1998

David Wilson, John Ashton and Douglas Sharp, *What Everyone in Britain Should Know About the Police*, Blackstone Press, 2001

The internet

http://www.criminal-justice-system.gov.uk/

A government web site which describes the various areas of the system in simple terms

http://www.scotland.gov.uk/library/documents/courts.htm

Gives an overview of the Scottish courts

http://www.sps.gov.uk/

The web site of the Scottish prison service. Gives an account of the daily routine in a Scottish prison plus lots of facts about the service.

http://www.independent.co.uk/search.jsp

The web site of the *Independent* newspaper where you can enter the topics you are interested in and find archive articles

http://www.guardian.co.uk/

A similar site for the *Guardian* newspaper

Visit www.learn.co.uk for more resources

To be read only by Gregory McTavish and his defence team:

You are innocent. The masks and gloves were for a bank raid you were planning the following week. You really were watching TV with your five friends who also had nothing to do with it. You have robbed banks before and have spent six years in prison for armed robbery. Your wife bought some of the numbered notes at a knock-down price thinking they were counterfeit. If you are convicted you will go to prison for a long time. You didn't buy the guns from Turner. He's lying to get remission (a reduction of his sentence). On the Sunday before the robbery you were at your nephew's christening with two hundred other people, and in the presence of a vicar.

Index